The Missions of California

Mission San Francisco de Solano

Allison Stark Draper

The Rosen Publishing Group's
PowerKids Press™
New York

For Jeff

Published in 2000 by The Rosen Publishing Group, Inc.
29 East 21st Street, New York, NY 10010

First Edition

Book Design: Danielle Primiceri

Photo Credits: pp. 1, 2, 16, 23, 42, 43, 44, 47, 48, 49, 51 © Cristina Taccone; pp. 6, 29, 30 © North Wind Picture Archive; p. 9 © Art Resource; pp. 12, 13, 20, 31, 46 © Michael K. Ward; pp. 14, 26, 27, 28 by Tim Hall; p. 17 © Seaver Center for Western History Research, Los Angeles County Museum of Natural History; p. 18 © The Bancroft Library; p. 39 © Archive Photos; p. 40 © The Granger Collection; p. 41B © N.Carter/North Wind Picture Archive; CORBIS-Bettmann; pp. 52, 57 © Christine Innamorato.

Editorial Consultant Coordinator: Karen Fontanetta, M.A., Curator, Mission San Miguel Arcángel
Editorial Consultant: Glenn E. Burch, State Park Historian, Sonoma, CA
Historical Photo Consultants: Thomas L. Davis, M. Div., M.A. and Michael K. Ward, M.A.

Draper, Allison Stark.
    Mission San Francisco de Solano / by Allison Stark Draper.
    p. cm. — (The missions of California)
    Includes index.
    Summary: Discusses the founding, building, operation, and closing of the Spanish mission in California's Valley of the Moon and its role in California history.
    ISBN: 0-8239-5507-9 (lib. bdg.)
    1. Mission San Francisco Solano (Sonoma, Calif.) —History Juvenile literature. 2. Spanish mission buildings—California—Sonoma Region—History Juvenile literature. 3. Franciscans—California—Sonoma Region—History Juvenile literature. 4. California—History—To 1846 Juvenile literature. 5. Indians of North America—Missions—California—Sonoma Region—History Juvenile literature. [1. Mission San Francisco Solano (Sonoma, Calif.) —History. 2. Missions—California. 3. Indians of North America—Missions—California. 4. California—History—To 1846.] I. Title. II. Series.
    F869.M654 D73 1999
    979.4'18—dc21

                        99-21447
                        CIP

Contents

The California Missions

The Valley of the Moon

In the vine-covered hills of Sonoma, California, there is a place called the Valley of the Moon. For thousands of years before the arrival of the Europeans, the American Indians who lived in the valley watched the path of the winter moon as it glowed and vanished seven times behind the black peaks of seven mountains before rising into the night sky.

In 1542, the Spanish claimed California, and in the mid-1700s, Spanish friars and soldiers began exploring this area. In 1823, when a friar named Fray José Altimira arrived in Sonoma, an Indian showed him the moon's path among the mountains and he gave the valley its name.

The Valley of the Moon is home to the town of Sonoma and Mission San Francisco de Solano (also known as Sonoma Mission). Founded in 1823 by Fray Altimira, Mission San Francisco de Solano is the last and most northern of the 21 Franciscan missions in California.

Why the Missions Were Built

The California missions were built in the late 1700s and early 1800s by Spanish Franciscan friars. These friars believed that it was their duty to convert the American Indians to Christianity in order to save their souls. Like most Europeans of their time, the friars believed that European customs and ideas were superior to those of the rest of the world. They thought that when the Indians had learned to live like Europeans, life for the Indians would improve. They wanted to teach the Indians about European ways of farming, raising animals, and worshiping God.

◀ *Mission San Francisco de Solano.*

Fray Junípero Serra

The first nine Franciscan missions in Alta California were built by a missionary named Fray Junípero Serra. Fray Serra was a brave explorer and a devout Christian. He founded the first mission, Mission San Diego de Alcalá, in 1769. After that, he created a chain of missions, along the coast of California. He built each mission 30 miles, or one day's journey, from the next. The road that links the missions is called El Camino Real, which means "The Royal Road" in Spanish. Mission San Francisco de Solano is the last mission on the northern end of El Camino Real.

Fray Serra and the other missionaries believed they were making the

world a better place. They believed once they had converted the Indians and taught them to be productive members of society, they could return the mission lands to the Indians to farm and rule as their own. However, as time passed, the missions were run with less care and respect for the Christian Indians, or neophytes. Whereas at first the Indians were nicely persuaded to join the missions, later they were forced to do so. At some missions, the neophytes were whipped or put

Fray Junípero Serra is known as the father of the missions.

in chains to stop them from running away. By the early 1800s, the missions were suffering terribly.

Fray José Altimira

Around this time, in 1820, Fray José Altimira sailed from Spain to Alta California. At the time, "California" consisted of what is now the state of California and the Baja Peninsula of Mexico. It was divided into Alta (upper) California and Baja (lower) California.

Fray Altimira was young, ambitious, and impatient for glory. He thought he would be more important than the great friar and mission founder Fray Serra. He dreamed of building a new mission on the far northern border of Alta California. On July 4, 1823, Fray Altimira founded the 21st and last California mission. He named it San Francisco de Solano and built it in the Valley of the Moon.

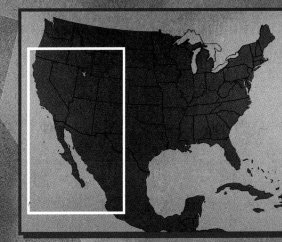

Alta California

Baja California

New Spain

The Spanish Explore the Americas

In 1492, an Italian sailor named Christopher Columbus sailed to the New World (North America, South America, and Central America). His expedition traveled in ships paid for by King Ferdinand and Queen Isabella of Spain. When he returned to Spain, he was a hero. Columbus published a map of his sea route, and shortly afterward, a Spanish soldier named Hernán Cortés followed it to the land now known as Mexico. At that time, the country was ruled by a rich and powerful people called the Aztecs. Cortés was an ambitious man and a strong leader. With only a small band of followers, he managed to conquer the Aztecs and claim their land and their gold for Spain. The Spanish called the Aztecs' country New Spain.

Cortés continued to explore the land to the west of the fallen Aztec Empire. In 1539, he sent a ship to explore the body of water separating New Spain from what he mistakenly thought was the island of Alta California. In 1540, an explorer named Vasquez de Coronado led a land expedition through the American Southwest, from what is now New Mexico to what is now Kansas. In 1542, another explorer, Juan Rodríguez Cabrillo, led a coastal expedition as far north as modern-day Oregon. None of these explorers found gold, rich farmland, or anything like the great empire of the Aztecs. As a result, Spain lost interest in northern exploration. Instead, for the next 200 years, they concentrated on settling New Spain.

The Decision to Settle in California

Finally, in the mid-1700s, Spain's interest in Alta California reawakened. The reason for this was that in 1741, the Russians landed

8

Ferdinand and Isabella seeing Christopher Columbus off from the dock at Palos, Spain on August 3, 1492. ▶

on the coast north of Alta California. When rumors of the Russian landing reached King Carlos III in Spain, he decided to strengthen his hold on the land. In 1768, he sent soldiers to the southern and northern ends of Alta California. He sent Franciscan friars with the soldiers to found missions and convert the American Indians to Christianity.

King Carlos III saw the founding of the missions as an important first step in turning Alta California into a Spanish colony. He wanted the missionaries to convert the American Indians because he knew that if the Indians spoke Spanish and considered themselves subjects of Spain, it would be harder for the Russians to move south and claim any of the land in Alta California for Russia.

Fray Serra's Expedition to Alta California

In 1768, King Carlos III sent an expedition to found the first mission in Alta California. Some of the explorers traveled by sea up the coast and some traveled overland from Baja California. The land party included 11 soldiers, 5 mule drivers, 12 Christian Indians, and a Franciscan friar named Fray Junípero Serra.

Fray Serra had lived in New Spain for almost 20 years, teaching Spanish, preaching, and converting Indians. He was deeply devoted to the cause of bringing Christianity to the Indians in Alta California. Fray Serra eventually founded nine of the missions in Alta California and became the first president of the mission system.

The First Mission

Fray Serra and his men arrived at the site of the first mission at the end of June. The mission was named Mission San Diego de Alcalá. The area was rich in fresh water and timber and there were large numbers of Indians living there. The local Indians were initially suspicious of the friars. In fact, during the whole year of 1769, the first year of the first mission in Alta California, not a single Indian converted to Christianity.

Despite their slow start at Mission San Diego de Alcalá, the friars did not lose hope. They had soldiers, weapons, and the Spanish Empire on their side. It was only a matter of time before they began to change the lives and the cultures of the Indians forever. The mission system, which would eventually stretch more than 500 hundred miles north to Mission San Francisco de Solano, had begun.

San Francisco de Solano

San Rafael Arcángel

San Francisco de Asís

San José

Santa Clara de Asís

Santa Cruz

San Juan Bautista

San Carlos Borromeo del Río Carmelo

Nuestra Señora de la Soledad

San Antonio de Padua

San Miguel Arcángel

San Luis Obispo de Tolosa

La Purísima Concepción

Santa Inés

Santa Bárbara

San Buenaventura

San Fernando Rey de España

San Gabriel Arcángel

San Juan Capistrano

San Luis Rey de Francia

San Diego de Alcalá

The American Indians

The Coast Miwok and the Pomo

The Indians at Mission San Francisco de Solano were mainly Coast Miwok and Pomo. The Coast Miwok lived on the peninsula across from San Francisco. The Pomo lived farther north. The lifestyles of the two tribes were very similar. They wore the same kind of feathered cloaks and caps. They built the same kind of earth-covered houses. They gathered and hunted the same kinds of food at the same time of year.

The dome shaped houses of the Pomo Indians.

They lived peacefully together before the arrival of the Spanish.

When the Spanish arrived, the Pomo had lived in the northern part of what became known as Alta California for more than 5,000 years. The Coast Miwok were probably in the region for 3,500 years.

No one knows for sure where they came from originally. Thousands of years ago, the land between Alaska and Russia was connected. People could travel on foot from Russia to Alaska and walk down the coast of what is now Canada into Alta California. It is possible that a little over 3,000 years ago, the Miwok came from the Ural mountains in Siberia, which is the eastern part of Russia.

Hunters and Gatherers

Before the Spanish arrived and introduced farming, the Pomo and

The Indians' houses were made of willow and tule thatch.

13

Fishing was an important source of food for the Indians.

Coast Miwok were hunters and gatherers. They treated the countryside as a huge, natural farm. They did not grow crops or raise animals. Instead, they used the plants, animals, and sea life that existed in the wild. They gathered *piñon* nuts in the mountains. They hunted deer in the forests. They fished for salmon in the rivers. They collected mussels and oysters from the ocean. In the fall and winter, they dug for mushrooms. In the spring, they gathered roots. In the summer, they ate greens and berries. Perhaps their most important food was acorns.

The Indians used the land without hurting it, so it could support them forever. They did not cut down forests, kill off whole animal populations, or create pollution. When droughts or rainy seasons destroyed certain types of plants, the Indians moved to different areas or collected different foods.

The European View of Indians

The Europeans were confused by the fact that the Indians had lived the same way for thousands of years. They saw that the Indians did not farm, raise animals, or build cities. They thought this meant that the Indians were less intelligent than the Europeans. The Spanish thought it was obvious that their methods of farming and raising livestock were superior to the hunting and gathering of the Indians. They did not think that hunting and gathering was an intelligent way of using the land.

What Became of the Indian Way of Life?

By the time Fray Altimira founded Mission San Francisco de Solano, the Franciscans had been in Alta California for 50 years. The Pomo and Coast Miwok who joined the mission knew much more about the Franciscans than many of the Indians who had joined earlier missions. In fact, many of the first Indians at Mission San Francisco de Solano were neophytes from Mission San Rafael Arcángel or Mission San Francisco de Asís (Mission Dolores). They knew more about mission life than about life in their own native tribes. In less than half a century, the European invasion had dramatically altered the native culture of Alta California.

Founding Mission
San Francisco de Solano

Trouble at Mission Dolores

By the early 1800s, Spanish territory in Alta California stretched from San Diego to San Francisco. Beyond San Francisco, the land still

▲

Mission Dolores in San Francisco.

belonged to the Indians. In 1820, Fray José Altimira sailed from Spain to join the friars at Mission Dolores in San Francisco. The mission was in terrible shape. The missionaries at Mission Dolores couldn't grow much food themselves because the mission soil was poor. The weather was cold and wet. Many neophytes were dying from European diseases, such as measles and tuberculosis. Many others left Mission Dolores for healthier, sunnier missions.

When Fray Altimira arrived, there were only 50 people working at Mission Dolores. Women were doing heavy fieldwork alongside the men. Fray Altimira wrote to the Mexican governor of Alta California, Don Luis Arguello, and told him that Mission Dolores was finished. Fray Altimira wanted to close the mission, take the neophytes and the supplies, and found a new mission farther north.

Fray Altimira's Quest for a New Mission

Governor Arguello gave Fray Altimira permission to build his mission because he liked the idea of establishing another northern settlement. One

Mission San Francisco de Solano. ▶

of Governor Arguello's duties was to protect the northern border of Alta California, because just north of there was a Russian settlement and fort.

Spain had been worried about the Russians ever since 1741 when they arrived in Alaska and King Carlos III feared they would start settling in Alta California. By 1812, the Russians had moved farther south. They had traveled down the coast by sea and bought a large piece of land just north of Alta California from the northern Indians. They paid for it in blankets, clothing, beads, and farm tools. Then they built a wooden settlement there named Fort Ross.

The Spanish believed that the Russians wanted to claim some part of the New World for Russia. As a result, the Spanish did not trust the Russians. As protection against the Spanish, the Russian fort was armed with 40 cannons and constantly guarded.

When Fray José Altimira decided to found a new mission in the north, he did not think about the Russians. He thought about the thousands of northern Indians he would convert to Christianity.

When Fray Altimira decided to found Mission San Francisco de Solano, he consulted Governor Arguello, but he did not consult Fray Señan, the Franciscan friar in charge of all the missions. Fray Señan was very ill and close to death at this time. When he

Fray Altimira founded Mission San Francisco de Solano.

learned that Fray Altimira planned to start a mission without consulting him, he was very angry. He informed Governor Arguello that neither he nor Fray Altimira had any power to start or close a mission.

Fray Vicente Sarría, who was soon to replace Fray Señan as president of the missions, convinced the dying friar to allow the founding of Mission San Francisco de Solano as long as Mission Dolores remained open, too. Fray Señan agreed. This meant that Fray Altimira had to build a whole new population of neophytes and find new materials and supplies.

Searching for the Perfect Mission Site

On June 25, 1823, Fray Altimira left San Francisco to find a site for his new mission. He was looking for a place with good farmland, plenty of water, and a large Indian population. He traveled with 24 soldiers and several neophytes. They sailed across the San Francisco Bay and landed near San Rafael. They walked north for 10 days. They climbed hills covered with grass and flowers. They hiked through thick forests and crossed cold rushing creeks. For dinner, they fried fresh fish and roasted bear meat.

When they reached Sonoma, they found rolling fields of rich farmland perfect for growing grapes. When they counted some 600 freshwater springs, Fray Altimira knew he had found the perfect place for his mission. On a slope near a gushing stream, he looked up at the sky, sifted a handful of dirt, and chose the site of the new mission. He named it San Francisco de Solano, for a missionary who had brought Christianity to many Indians in Peru.

Building the Mission

Blessing the Site at Sonoma

On July 4, 1823, Fray Altimira rose at dawn to bless the site at Sonoma. He cut down a tree, made it into a cross, and planted the cross in the earth. He read from the Bible, sang hymns, and prayed. The soldiers shot their guns in honor of the new mission. Mission San Francisco de Solano was born.

Construction Begins

On August 25, 1823, Fray Altimira and a small group of neophyte laborers began to build Mission San Francisco de Solano at Sonoma. Twelve soldiers stood guard to protect them. The mission's general design consisted of long buildings built in the shape of a square. This is called a quadrangle. A church was built in one corner of the quadrangle, and residences, workshops, a kitchen, and a storage area completed the square shape.

Surrounding this, they built a long, low wooden structure plastered inside and out with whitewashed mud to serve as living quarters for the neophytes. Beside this, they planted fields of crops and orchards. There was also grazing land for their livestock.

For the soldiers, they built a series of *palizadas* out of poles tied together with cowhide, coated with mud, and thatched with tule, a type of reed. For the friars, they built an adobe, or clay-brick, house roofed with tiles.

The Spanish Californians liked to build with adobe because it stays cool in the summer and warm in the winter. Unlike wood, however, it needs to be shaped into bricks and hardened by the sun or in an oven

The Indians and friars used adobe to build the mission.

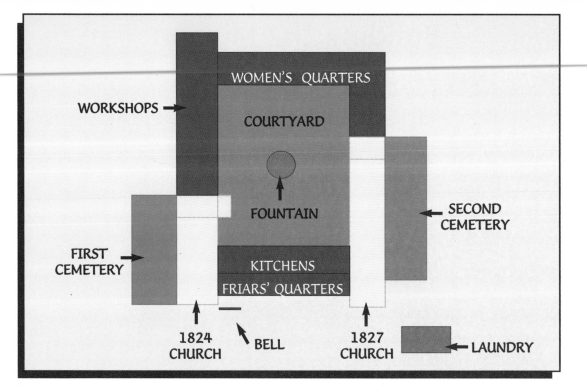

WORKSHOPS →

WOMEN'S QUARTERS

COURTYARD

FOUNTAIN →

SECOND CEMETERY ←

FIRST CEMETERY →

KITCHENS

FRIARS' QUARTERS

1824 CHURCH

BELL ↖

1827 CHURCH

← LAUNDRY

before it can be used. Due to Fray Altimira's impatience, he decided to start building before the adobe bricks were hardened. As a result, two unroofed adobe structures fell apart in an unexpected rainstorm. Fray Altimira waited for the rain to stop and immediately rebuilt them.

By the spring, the mission had a brand new, whitewashed wooden church. In 1824, Fray Altimira held an official dedication day. Fray Sarría gave the mission a painting of San Francisco de Solano, the patron saint of their new mission. Fray Altimira hung it in the place of honor above the altar.

The Russians at Fort Ross gave generously to the new mission. They sent vases, hammered brass basins, hand-carved bookstands, picture frames, candles, handwoven linens, embroidered silk veils for the tabernacle, and Mass bells. The friars at Mission Dolores sent 3,000 sheep, 60 horses, 50 cows, 40 oxen, and many farming tools.

Fray Altimira continued to expand the mission. He built a granary and new wooden buildings for the soldiers and their families. He also built several larger adobe buildings where the missionaries and neophytes studied and worked. One was 120 feet long and 30 feet wide. It had a corridor and a tiled roof. In 1825, the neophytes completed another long wing of living quarters for the friars.

In 1826, Fray Altimira was replaced by Fray Buenaventura Fortuni. Fray Fortuni made many improvements to the mission. He laid the foundations for a large, permanent church. He also built a stone water tank or cistern in the middle of the courtyard. The missionaries were able to pump water from the river into the cistern. That meant they no longer had to walk back and forth to the river with buckets. They used the cistern water for drinking, washing, cooking, and laundry.

The tiled roof of the workshops.

Daily Life at the Mission

Unlike the hunting and gathering life of the Pomo and Coast Miwok Indians, which changed from day to day and season to season, mission life was exactly the same every day except Sunday. The friars offered the Indians regular meals, sleeping quarters, and, when they died, salvation in heaven. In return, the Indians worked in the fields and learned to be Christians.

At the missions, the Indians' lives were controlled by bells that rang when it was time to wake, eat, work, and sleep. The Indians did have some free time for games and relaxation right before sleep, but in general they were allowed little time to pursue any of their former activities, such as hunting or traditional crafts that did not serve the missionaries.

Everybody at the mission ate a morning porridge made of corn, called *atole*. For dinner they ate a thick stew of corn, meat, wheat, peas, and beans, called *pozole*. They did all of the work needed to feed, clothe, and house all of the people at the mission.

At Mission San Francisco de Solano, after building sleeping quarters for the soldiers and the friars, the neophytes began working in the fields. They cut down trees and prepared the soil for planting. To make an orchard, they planted 300 fruit trees. To make a vineyard, they grew 3,000 vines of purple grapes.

For meals at the mission, the Indians grew beans, peas, and lentils and planted large fields of wheat, corn, and barley. In addition to working in the fields, they tended the horses and cattle that grazed in the pastures and fattened hogs in pens. They raised sheep for meat and wool. Fray Altimira set up a large, Spanish-style loom and taught the

One of the mission bells. ▶

▲

Cattle were very important at the missions. They could be used to work in the fields and they could be sold for their meat, hide, and tallow.

American Indians to weave woolen cloth. They wove carpets, blankets, and clothing. They also set up a blacksmith shop and made horseshoes, spurs, nails, and tools.

Cattle-raising was very profitable because of the trade in cattle hide and tallow. Tallow was made from cattle fat and used to make candles and soap. The gentle climate and rich grasslands of Alta California made it so easy to raise cattle that cattle hides became known as "California bank notes." By selling cattle hide and tallow, the missionaries were able to buy manufactured goods from the United States, Europe, and Asia. They bought coffee, sugar, tobacco, farm tools, and fine decorations for the church.

Discontentment and Disease

Life at Mission San Francisco de Solano was not always happy or healthy. Although the friars wanted to help the Indians, they were simply unable to. They did not understand that the American Indians deserved to live the way they always had. They did not understand why so many Indians felt as though they were being imprisoned.

When the Europeans came to Alta California, they unknowingly brought many diseases with them, such as measles and influenza. Some of these diseases were not particularly deadly in Europe, but they were often deadly to the Indians, who were not immune to them. Some of these illnesses were so widespread that the entire Indian population of Alta California declined by 90 percent in the first 100 years of European settlement.

Another problem for the Indians at Mission San Francisco de Solano was that Fray Altimira was a cruel man. When the neophytes disobeyed him, he whipped and imprisoned them. There were always some Indians trying to escape from the mission, but soldiers were sent out after them. Eventually, the Indians lost patience with Fray Altimira. In 1826, a large group of Indians attacked the mission. They looted and burned the buildings. They forced Fray Altimira and the few neophytes who stood by him to flee for their lives. Not long afterward, Fray Altimira left Alta California forever and sailed back to Spain.

Many Indians became sick and died from European diseases.

The Fall of the Mission

The Friars

After Fray José Altimira was driven from Mission San Francisco de Solano, his work was continued by Fray Buenaventura Fortuni. Fray Fortuni treated the neophytes with respect. Many Indians who had left the mission out of disgust with Fray Altimira returned to welcome Fray Fortuni. Under Fray Fortuni's guidance, the mission reached the height of its success. In 1830, nearly 1,000 Indians lived at the mission.

When Fray Fortuni retired in 1833, he was replaced by the insensitive Fray José Gutierrez. The Indians did not like Fray Gutierrez. Many of them left for other missions or vanished into the hills to rejoin Indian tribes. Fray Gutierrez left Mission San Francisco de Solano after a year and a half. The next friar, Fray Lorenzo Quíjas, arrived just as the Mexican government put an end to the mission system.

The Secularization of the Missions

During the early 1800s, Spain had control of California and New Spain (what we now call Mexico). The Mexicans, however, were fighting to regain control of their land. In 1821, Mexico won independence from Spain, taking control of California.

The Mexicans had very different ideas from the Spanish about what to do with the missions. In 1834, the Mexican government passed laws to secularize

Map of New Spain.

Many Indians left Mission San Francisco de Solano because Fray Altimira mistreated them.

29

the missions, which meant that the missions were no longer under the financial control of the Catholic Church. Most of the Franciscan missionaries were sent back to Spain and replaced with special priests called *curas*, who did not do missionary work. Secularization of the missions also meant that the Indians were free to leave.

The Mission Lands

▲ Lieutenant Mariano Vallejo.

Many of the missions fell apart after secularization. A plan was made to divide the mission lands between the neophytes and the settlers. However, corrupt officials and greedy settlers found a way around this and took the land for themselves. Most of the mission lands at Mission San Francisco de Solano were taken over by Lieutenant Mariano Vallejo. Vallejo grew rich and powerful working the land at Mission San Francisco de Solano. He eventually became an important general.

What Happened to the Indians?

Some Indians could not understand how the land could be taken away from them. Laws of ownership were foreign to them. Other Indians did not want to stay and farm the land but wanted to return to their villages or to the bands of Indian revolutionaries forming in the mountains. Other Indians remained behind because they had no other place to go. Their villages no longer existed, their ways of hunting and

After the missions were secularized, some Indians were able to return to their villages.

gathering were lost, and their rituals and languages forgotten. Their tribal leaders had been killed off or had gone into hiding. The American Indians had lost their culture and now their lands. This meant that their newfound freedom did not make their lives any better than they had been at the missions.

The neophytes who did remain at Mission San Francisco de Solano (which was now a parish and not a true mission) found it almost impossible to run without the organization of the mission friars. As a result, many of them were left homeless. Some worked for General Vallejo or other local ranchers. Some found low-paying jobs working in shops, as house servants, or caring for European children.

Indian Uprisings

In the years after Mexico's revolt against Spain, there were more and more Indian uprisings. By the 1820s and 1830s, groups of Indians were banding together. They formed small armies and began raiding the ranchers' homes. They saw the ranchers as the invading enemies who had stolen their land from them. The ranchers were forced to take the Indian raiders more and more seriously. Sometimes they had to fight back with forces of 100 soldiers or more.

The Indians were dangerous raiders because they were very good horseback riders. In addition to farming and Christianity, the Spanish had introduced the Indians to two important skills: the use of guns and horseback riding. When the Indians first saw Spaniards on horseback, they thought they were a new creature, half-human and half-horse. They had never thought to tame the horses that ran wild in the Alta California

The Indians revolted against the ranchers who treated them unfairly.

33

Unique Features of the Mission

General Mariano Vallejo and Chief Sum-yet-ho

In the 1830s and 1840s, two of the most powerful men in Alta California lived in the Valley of the Moon. General Mariano Vallejo was the wealthy rancher who had taken over the mission lands at Mission San Francisco de Solano. Directly south of him, Chief Sum-yet-ho, or Mighty Arm, was a Suisune Indian chief. Sum-yet-ho was six feet, seven inches tall. General Vallejo was afraid of the chief's growing strength among the American Indians. He decided to attack him while he was still sure he could defeat him.

General Vallejo gathered his soldiers and met Chief Sum-yet-ho and his army in Suscol Valley. The bows, arrows, and spears of the Indians were no match for the guns and swords of the Mexicans. General Vallejo was victorious. Despite the defeat, Chief Sum-yet-ho liked Vallejo. They eventually became allies and friends. Chief Sum-yet-ho learned to speak Spanish and often visited Vallejo at his ranch.

General Vallejo and the Missions

General Vallejo was responsible for keeping the peace at the local missions and with the Indian chieftains. In 1833, the year before secularization, he dealt with Fray Gutierrez at Mission San Francisco de Solano and Fray Jesus Mercado at Mission San Rafael Arcángel. Both men were difficult, unkind, and disliked by the Indians.

A few months after Fray Mercado's arrival, he arrested a group of Indians on false charges of stealing. He then sent out his own armed converts at night to attack them. Twenty-one Indians were killed, and an equal number were wounded. General Vallejo had to go to the

General Vallejo helped to keep the peace at Mission San Francisco de Solano. ▶

mission, release the captives, and calm the remaining Indians.

After this, General Vallejo combined Mission San Francisco de Solano and Mission San Rafael Arcángel under the control of Fray Lorenzo Quíjas. This did not help matters as Fray Quíjas dealt poorly with the Indians and fought with General Vallejo. Finally, under orders from the government, General Vallejo closed both missions. He divided some of the flocks and herds among the remaining neophytes and kept the rest for himself.

General Vallejo was not a religious man, but he kept up the church at Mission San Francisco de Solano. He added a tower for the bells, and he furnished a room in the friars' quarters for a priest. However, after secularization, he could not find a Franciscan friar to live and work at Mission San Francisco de Solano.

General Vallejo knew many Indians and had several allies among the local chiefs. Once an Indian chief came to visit him in the winter. The Indian was not a Christian and did not wear European clothes. He was almost entirely naked. "Aren't you cold?" asked the general. "Is your face cold?" asked the Indian. "No," answered the general. The chief smiled and pointed to his body. "I am all face."

The Bear Flag Revolt

During the 1840s, many American settlers heard a rumor that there was free land in California and moved out to claim it. The Mexican government, however, refused to allow Americans to own land in California. The Americans became frustrated and angry. In the summer of 1846, a band of Americans decided to challenge the Mexicans. They called themselves Osos, or bears. The Osos chose Mission San Francisco de Solano as the site of their revolt.

▲

The Bear Flag Revolt.

At dawn on June 14, 1846, thirty-three heavily armed Osos rode into Sonoma. They stopped in front of General Mariano Vallejo's adobe mansion and pounded on the door. They demanded that the general come out and surrender. Vallejo put on his uniform, opened the door, and invited them in for breakfast. General Vallejo knew Mexico was too weak to rule a place as large and rich as California. He told the Americans he would join them. They believed him, but they still arrested him.

The Osos declared Sonoma the capital of the Republic of California. They decided to make a new Californian flag and raise it in Sonoma Plaza. They drew a grizzly bear on a piece of white cloth and wrote "California Republic" in black letters across the middle. The grizzly became the symbol of the new Bear Flag Republic. It is still the symbol of California today.

▲

The raising of the California Republic flag.

The Republic of California lasted for 25 days. On July 7, 1846, the American government claimed all of California for the United States. The Osos agreed to join the other Americans. They lowered the Bear Flag and raised the Stars and Stripes.

American flag from 1846. ▶

◀ *California Republic flag.*

Mission San Francisco de Solano Today

Mission San Francisco de Solano came to a temporary end in 1881 when the church and the friars' quarters were sold and used to store hay for 30 years. Wine was stored in the cloisters. Later, the church became a blacksmith's shop.

In 1903, as the walls began to crumble, the California Landmarks League was able to save the mission. They collected $13,000, bought the mission, and gave it to the state of California. In 1911, repairs began, and in October 1922, the mission opened as a museum. The oldest surviving building is the wing of the friars' quarters that Fray José Altimira built in 1825. It stands just east of the present chapel. A large bell that disappeared from the mission in 1881 was found in a museum in San Francisco by the Sonoma Women's Club. They brought it back and hung it in front of the mission.

Anvil used by blacksmiths at Mission San Francisco de Solano.

Today, Mission San Francisco de Solano sits in the center of the town of Sonoma. Sonoma Plaza, the huge shaded square designed by General Mariano Vallejo, is surrounded by shops, restaurants, and historic adobe buildings. The old Mexican army barracks are still there along with some of the nineteenth-century hotels. General Vallejo's house on the plaza, La Casa Grande, is now a museum. Half a mile to the northwest, his house has been restored to look as though he might

Mission San Francisco de Solano today.

▲

The old Mexican army barracks.

SONOMA BARRACKS

Grapevines at Sonoma, California.

sweep through the door at any moment.

Sonoma, in the Valley of the Moon, is now best known as the birthplace of California wine making. Fray José Altimira planted the first grapes in Sonoma to make wines for Mass. Today, Sonoma wines are tasted all over the world.

The Pomo and Coast Miwok Indians Today

As for the Pomo and Coast Miwok Indians, who suffered so much at the hands of the Europeans, there are currently fewer than 50 full-blooded survivors. Yet the California Indians have survived. They have

The Spanish friars believed that bringing Christianity to the Indians was a great gift.

kept many of their ancient traditions. They have protected burial sites and sacred places. They have reclaimed some of their land.

In the 1960s, Indian activists from all over the United States began working to change the way the history of the American Indians is taught in schools. They created departments of Native American Studies at colleges and universities. They revised school textbooks to explain history from the Indian point of view, as well as from the European point of view.

The missions that still stand today help to show the two very different points of view of the Franciscans and the American Indians. They show the good intentions of the Spanish friars who believed that bringing Christianity to the Indians was a great gift. They also show how the

▲

A school field trip to Mission San Francisco de Solano.

mission system stole the Indians' land and culture, caused them much suffering, and cost them many lives.

The pre-European American Indian side of the story in California is harder to see. It is not recorded in stone buildings and wooden forts. It is not as obvious as General Vallejo's ranch house or the great iron bell of Mission San Francisco de Solano. It is not as easy to visit as the Mexican barracks or the nineteenth-century hotels. It lives on in places like the seasonal routes of the hunters and gatherers. It lives on in the bright and dark path of the moon in the winter as it passes behind the seven mountain peaks at the northern border of the Valley of the Moon.

Views of the mission courtyard. ▶

Artifacts found at Mission San Francisco de Solano (clockwise from top left): cannon, eating utensils and bowls, sleeping quarters, and wagon.

Mission Recipe

(Please ask an adult for help before heating the stove!)

Champurrado (cocoa)

In the mission days, the Spanish Californians liked to drink this very thick and sweet hot chocolate that they called champurrado (cham-per-RAHD-oh).

3 teaspoons cocoa

3 teaspoons sugar

1/2 cup hot water

2 1/2 cups milk, scalded

1 pinch cinnamon

1 tablespoon cornstarch

1 well beaten egg

1 teaspoon vanilla

Combine the chocolate and sugar over low heat and add the hot water slowly. Stir until the mixture forms a smooth paste. Slowly add the milk and cornstarch and, just before serving, fold in the eggs, vanilla, and cinnamon.

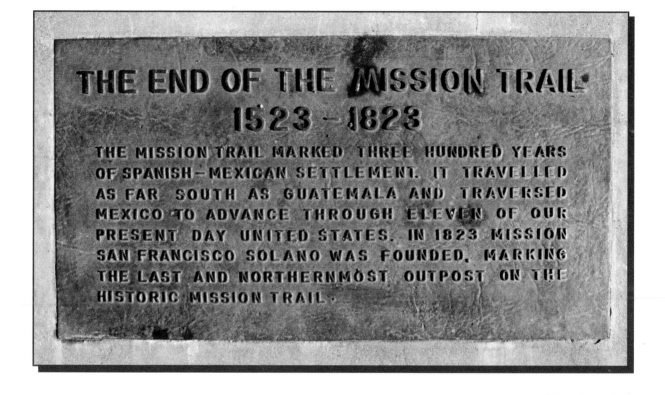

THE END OF THE MISSION TRAIL
1523 - 1823

THE MISSION TRAIL MARKED THREE HUNDRED YEARS OF SPANISH – MEXICAN SETTLEMENT. IT TRAVELLED AS FAR SOUTH AS GUATEMALA AND TRAVERSED MEXICO TO ADVANCE THROUGH ELEVEN OF OUR PRESENT DAY UNITED STATES. IN 1823 MISSION SAN FRANCISCO SOLANO WAS FOUNDED, MARKING THE LAST AND NORTHERNMOST OUTPOST ON THE HISTORIC MISSION TRAIL.

As indicated by this sign, the mission system spread way beyond California, as far south as Guatemala. Mission San Francisco de Solano marks the end of the mission trail.

Make Your Own
Mission San Francisco de Solano

To make your own model of the San Francisco de Solano mission, you will need:

foamcore board
string
scissors
cardboard
Popsicle sticks
fake flowers/trees

sand
paint (white, brown)
ruler
X-Acto knife (ask for
  an adult's help)

masking tape
paintbrush
glue

Directions

Step 1: Cut a 20" by 20" piece of foamcore to use as the base of your mission.

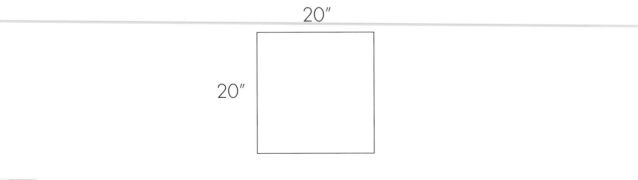

20"

20"

Adult supervision is suggested.

Step 2: Make the front and back of the large church by cutting out two cardboard pieces. They should be 8" wide, 9" high at the peak, and 8" high at the sides.

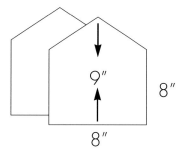

Step 3: Cut a door in the front of the church and a window above the door.

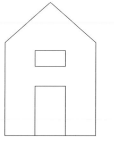

Step 4: Cut two side walls that measure 8" by 8".

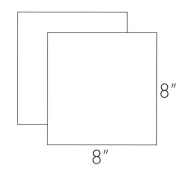

Step 5: Tape the front, back, and sides of the church together. Attach the mission church to the base.

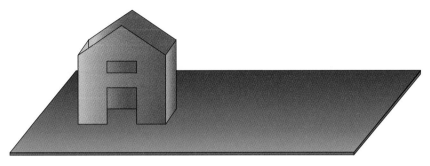

Step 6: Make two mission quadrangle walls that measure 5" by 4". Tape these so they stick out from the front and back of the mission church.

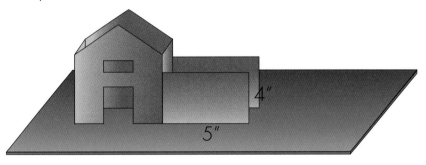

Step 7: To make the front and back of the small church, cut two pieces that measure 4" wide by 7" high at the peak, and 6" high at the sides. Cut out doors and windows.

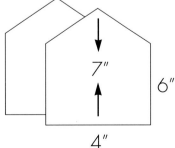

Step 8: Make two side walls for the small church that measure 8″ by 6″. Tape the front, back, and side walls together.

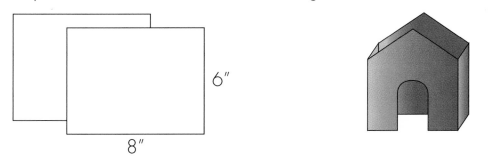

6″

8″

Step 9: Attach the small church and the quadrangle walls to the base. Mix sand and white paint together. Paint the mission with this mixture.

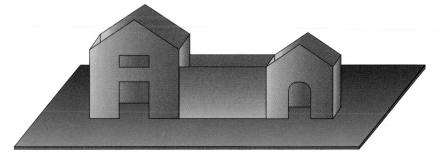

Step 10: To make the roof of the large church, cut out a 9″ by 9″ piece of cardboard and fold it in half.

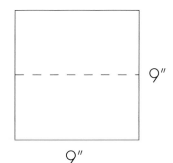

9″

9″

Step 11: Paint the roof brown and glue it to the top of the large church.

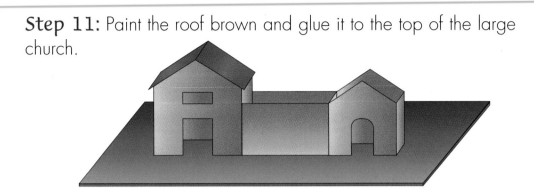

Step 12: Cut a 5" by 9" piece of cardboard for the small church roof. Fold it in half, lengthwise. Paint it and attach it to the small church.

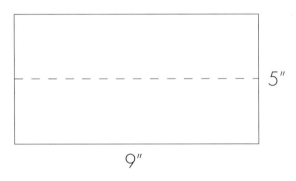

5"

9"

Step 13: Break a Popsicle stick in half, lengthwise, and then into smaller pieces. Paint pieces brown and glue above the church doors and windows.

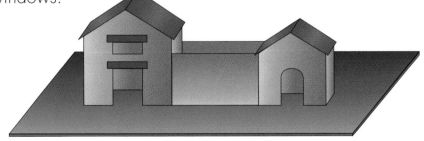

Step 14: To make the bell holder, cut Popsicle sticks to 3" and paint brown. Glue together and stick into the foamcore. Hang a bell with string or wire.

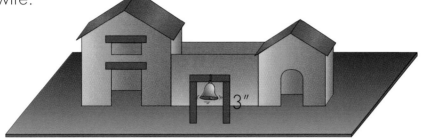

Step 15: Add trees and flowers to decorate the mission grounds.

*Use the above mission as a reference for building your mission.

Important Dates in Mission History

1492	Christopher Columbus reaches the West Indies
1542	Cabrillo's expedition to California
1602	Sebastián Vizcaíno sails to California
1713	Fray Junípero Serra is born
1769	Founding of San Diego de Alcalá
1770	Founding of San Carlos Borromeo del Río Carmelo
1771	Founding of San Antonio de Padua and San Gabriel Arcángel
1772	Founding of San Luis Obispo de Tolosa
1775–76	Founding of San Juan Capistrano
1776	Founding of San Francisco de Asís
1776	Declaration of Independence is signed
1777	Founding of Santa Clara de Asís
1782	Founding of San Buenaventura
1784	Fray Serra dies
1786	Founding of Santa Bárbara Virgen y Mártir
1787	Founding of La Purísima Concepción de Maria Santísima
1791	Founding of Santa Cruz and Nuestra Señora de la Soledad
1797	Founding of San José, San Juan Bautista, San Miguel Arcángel, and San Fernando Rey de España
1798	Founding of San Luis Rey de Francia
1804	Founding of Santa Inés Virgen y Mártir
1817	Founding of San Rafael Arcángel
1823	**Founding of San Francisco de Solano**
1848	Gold found in northern California
1850	California becomes the 31st state

Glossary

activists (AK-tih-vists) People who take action for what they believe is right.

adobe (uh-DOH-bee) Sun-dried bricks made of mud and straw.

allies (AL-yz) People, groups, or nations who unite for a special purpose.

claim (KLAYM) When a person takes something and says it belongs to him or her.

conquered (KON-kerd) Defeated in a war.

convert (kun-VIRT) To change a person's religious beliefs.

devout (dih-VOWT) Religious and active in worship and prayer.

founded (FOWN-ded) When a place has been established or started.

Franciscan (fran-SIS-kin) A member of a Catholic religious group started by Saint Francis of Assisi in 1209.

granary (GRAY-nar-ee) A windowless building used for storing grain.

looted (LOO-ted) To rob, especially in a war or violent situation.

Glossary

missionaries (MIH-shuh-nayr-eez) People who teach their religion to people with different beliefs.

neophytes (NEE-oh-fyts) American Indians who became Christians and lived at the missions.

peninsula (peh-NIN-suh-lah) A piece of land almost completely surrounded by water.

revolutionaries (reh-vuh-LOO-shuh-nayr-eez) People who want to overthrow a government.

sacred (SAY-kred) Of great religious importance.

salvation (sal-VAY-shun) The saving of a person's soul.

secularization (seh-kyoo-luh-rih-ZAY-shun) A process by which the mission lands were made to be non-religious.

tule (TOO-lee) Reeds used by Indians to make houses or boats.

Pronunciation Guide

atole (ah-TOL-ay)

El Camino Real (EL kah-MEE-noh RAY-al)

José Altimira (hoe-ZAY al-tih-MEER-ah)

José Gutierrez (hoe-ZAY goo-tee-YAIR-ez)

Juan Ybarra (WAHN ee-BAR-ah)

Junípero Serra (joo-NIH-peh-ro SER-ah)

La Casa Grande (lah KAH-sah GRAHN-day)

Lorenzo Quíjas (lo-REN-zoh KEE-hahs)

Mariano Vallejo (mar-ee-AHN-oh vy-YAY-ho)

Miwok (MEE-wahk)

palizadas (pah-lee-ZAH-daz)

piñon (peen-YOHN)

Pomo (POE-moe)

pozole (poh-ZOHL-ay)

Resources

To learn more about the California missions, check out these books and Web sites:

Books:

Fray Junípero Serra: The Traveling Missionary by Linda Lyngheim
Vallejo by Esther J. Comstock

Web Sites:

http://www.sonomavalley.com/mission.html
http://www.steindesign.com/mitch_home_pg/max_mission_page/mission.html
http://www.sfmuseum.org/bio/vallejo.html
http://coyote.rain.org/~serra/serra.htm
http://tqd.advanced.org/3615/tour3.html

Index